THAT STRANGER

love & best wishes
from

Jack

xxx

James Keery

THAT STRANGER, THE BLUES

CARCANET

Acknowledgements

Grateful acknowledgement is made to the editors of the following
periodicals, in which some of these poems have appeared:
*The Echo Room, folded sheets, The Green Book, The Honest Ulsterman,
The Independent, joe soap's canoe, Krax, The North, Odyssey, Ore,
Other Poetry, PN Review, Poetica, The Rialto, Seam, Slow Dancer,
Smiths Knoll, Staple* and *The Wide Skirt.*
'Your Sister's Good Hair' makes use of letters in the four volumes
of John Byrom's *Remains* (Chetham Society, 1854-7). Other poems
make use of 'found' material from various sources.

First published in 1996 by
Carcanet Press Limited
402-406 Corn Exchange Buildings
Manchester M4 3BY

A CIP catalogue record for this book
is available from the British Library
ISBN 1 85754 231 2

The publisher acknowledges financial assistance
from the Arts Council of England

Set in 10 pt Bembo by Bryan Williamson, Frome
Printed and bound in England by SRP Ltd, Exeter

Contents

Steppin' Out: Nocturne

Nigh upon that hour
When the lone hern forgets his melancholy,
Lets down his other leg,
And steps into the dark water up to his ankles,
I closed an old green edition of Tennyson's
Poems in which I was making pensive marks,
Got into my dufflecoat, and went out for a walk, past Crow Wood.
The thaw soaked the fields, but the floods
Had gone, leaving the pathways
Greasy, half-refrozen.

They were skating on the Oxide,
Brian and John, but the scarves and snowballs
Weather withdrew too quickly.
I passed where Marie had finished with me
After a visit to the ice-rink.
I tried to locate our secret path, only to encounter
One of those red-and-white barriers, vertical:
'It can't be empowered to drop on someone just...'

Well, you go to a party,
And you laugh loud and hearty –
You stay all night, you know you make the scene,
As you go steppin' out queen...

Cathy

Ah, Cathy, with loose flaxen tresses,
Pale skin, and contemptuous lips!
Her mother's sad Irish distraction
Packed all of her folk off in ships,

And Cathy and she are at daggers
And Cathy she can't take much more.
Already she's lying and drinking,
And Karen calls Cathy a whore.

Cathy

I stepped from the bus
And there was Cathy,
As if to meet me!

Last January,
In the mocking snow
By the police-
Station, I
Gazed after her
Glance:
Now,
By the bus-
Stop, just
Opposite the police-
Station, my
Fortune washes Cathy
Up to my feet.

The sea of time and space
Thundered!
Cathy looks up to my eyes,
Amused,
Shepherding black-
Polythene
Bags with Shelley,
To confront me
With my dream
Of seventeen!

'Where are you going?'
'To Maureen's.'
We acquainted,
Almost shyly.
I'd heard tidings
From Karen.
'Ah,' she smiled,
'I don't do anything bad.'

Necessary Laziness

Lo Catoun, which that was so wys a man,
Seyde he nat thus, *Ne do no fors of dremes*?

I have dreamed lately serene-blue unsolipsistic dreams,
Slumbering off the passive exhausting delirium of flu.
A mere fever of thyself, Keats would call me,
But my own life seems a bit less real than other people's
Just at the moment; I am one
Of those to whom the impressions of the world
Are beautiful and will not let them rest:
A vision of the progress of an essay
Which I have never waking contemplated
But on which Susan
Is presently intent
Blended into walking down Culcheth Hall Drive
With Alison, passing the house
Of a neighbour and his wife (who don't exist)
Exchanging with her the smile of a free equal
And making a casual promise to the flags!

St Patrick's Day

Maureen was intrigued.
I called at Blair Walk –
Cathy was out.
Quite by chance
I'd come upon her,
Packing up rails
Of leather coats
In the empty market.

Distractions of March

Come out, come out, you yellow daffs,
Flying high on your long green staffs!

It gave over just as it was winning.
I'd stood at the kitchen window watching each flake land
And melt into the slice of Dunn's tree.
It dampened and coated the red wood, but on the path
Began to collect in puddles and drowned itself.
I felt in my heart somehow it wouldn't lie, and continued washing up.
The afternoon grows deeper, and flakes still fall, but the snow has not
Established the soft limits of desolation. It lies
Too wetly on the lawn, weaker and weaker, going green and patiently
Expecting a bright moon to freeze the air,
Which it just might. Snow-besprinkled daffodils, less
Wintry than that east wind, that blew all yesterday,
When Steve caught the plane to Kathmandu, until July. He was
    considering
Buying a house in Cambridge, according to Susan.
Melinda's stuck with her dissertations.
I saw a great tit shrug some snow off its wings.

Eclipse

Not every cloud has a silver lining, of course,
But a continental black one that has has
Intervened between the sun and our afternoon.
The trees are suddenly black against the blue.

Extraordinary Days

It had frozen, the snow was fluffy,
Dry, not sugary. The moon was full.
It looked like a proof crown
In the drifting slush
Above water of silver blue.
And this afternoon the grass
Not even wet underfoot
As I walk the same fields. I find
Typing hot work this weather.
The sunlight dazzles the keys,
Warms my bare arms,
Fringes my eyes with green contentment.

Winter Hill looked almost Alpine,
Snow-flanked in the blue air.
Today was blustery, sleety;
I looked at photographs till I was cold.
John's birthday's soon.
March comes in like a lion,
Goes out like a lamb;
I hope it's springy in the morning
When I hitch down.
I had a headache, but Mum and I
Typed up the application amicably,
Between coffees and Co-op apple pies.

Ainsdale Beach

Ad domnulam suam

We never even reached
The distant sea,
Our feet
Benumbed and red,
The vast sand
Sluiced by rivers
Which I carried you across,
Your body
Slim and sturdy
In my arms.

You tucked the hems
Of your dresses
Into your knickers.

I wouldn't let Alaine
Pick daffodils.

Your hand
On my shoulder,
My arm round you,
Alaine
Importuning me
Bitterly
To stay,
I was the proudest person
In the city –
From Widnes
To the Belfast Docks!

Angela

I got two pints of milk and an apple pie,
And coming back met Angela, who smiled –
'I haven't seen you for a long time!'

Why couldn't I have been smart and clean?
I look forward to meeting her, and when I
Luckily do, my hair is blowing in my eyes,

My clothes are stale. She wanted to know
Which house was ours. I might, if
I hadn't been so down, have asked her in.

Buckets of Rain

I'd walked through the temporary market under the precinct,
Half-reluctant to see Cathy, which I didn't,
But it was worth it just to see Susan and Alaine.
Susan modelled her sash for the Glorious Twelfth.
Someone had been hit by a brick at the parade,
Just outside the Orange Lodge.
Alaine said it was her birthday,
But I reminded her that she'd been born on cup-final day.
'I watched the game on TV.
I can still remember Astle's goal,
And I thought the action replay was number two!
Alaine made up for that, though, didn't she?'
Alaine glanced at her father,
Who had had her christened after Alan Ball.
She and Susan and Donna were singing a rhyme
About Dallas,
>   *I'm only a poor little Ewing,*
>   *JR keeps on picking on me . . .*
I asked them where they had got it,
But all they would say
Was that they had made it up themselves.
We stared through the square holes in the pavement
At the carriageway below,
And I explained the Heineken poster to Susan.
We took a walk down to the Pier Head
And emptied the swinging buckets on the abstract fountain.
It came on rain again as I was seeing them home.

Harvest Moon

I watch my brisk shadow cross the nettles,
And seem to see the willow herb purple again,
Though it's fluffy and almost flowerless.
The moon is actually too bright to look at.

Blue summer has reserved late August,
And the silver lapwing, whose nest
I never noticed amongst the green blades,
Raises a shriek of protest over the sheaves.

Idyll

Do not go gentle into the blackberry night
So affects my muse now a chaste fallowness
The pale yellow sun remains outside
Pretentious masqueradings of young egotists?
No wit like bought wit, Melinda!
The constant anxiety over looks
The art of teaching fish by slow degrees
To live without water
And if I drink oblivion of a day
So shorten I the stature of my soul
A press of lilies that have silver ears
The cameos we rescue out of dreams
Mooching rhetorical among purple leaves
Sei una putana, Veronica!
Corresponsive and fulfilling bolts
And all its metal bent for a paltry song!
He persisted in his overestimation of classrooms
This theme calls me in sleep
I announce the justification of candour
And the justification of pride
He says your contempt for him is to some extent justified
Well it is
We produce persons with cultivated graces
To dignify our voracity
Worry is a feeble muse, Melinda!
A furnace in an otherwise quiet sky
The green floods of mud shine, and the brown
Grass that's overgrown the stubble darkens.

Perspicuous Weather

The weather was like a new pin this afternoon.
A strict illusion brings the loose patrol
Across the field of February mud.

The dangers seem distant over the grey horizon.
Crocuses have come out, and the middle ground
Is beginning to take solid form under my feet.

Laze Laze Pick Pick Pick

'Oh, I've got that book of yours, *The Pigman*, I'll get it.'
'Did you like it?' 'No. I couldn't stand it, to be honest.'
'It goes down very well in class.' 'Mmm...I don't think
Much of it, though, do you?' 'Mm, as a kids' book...it's not
My favourite, but I'd recommend it.' 'Mmm...Do you read
To them a lot, or do you let them read by themselves?' 'I do
Read to them quite a bit. They're EFL, remember.' 'You don't
Get them to write, then?' 'Well, as I say...' 'Yeah. You're
Not into kids' poetry, really, are you?' 'I don't think it
Should necessarily be in *The Oxford Book*.' 'You think it's
Rubbish?' 'No, I don't think that, just that it tends to be,
Well, accidental, that's all.' 'Listen, you were talking
About "Freudian poems from little girls", do you want to have
A look at one that really is?' 'I'll look at one.' 'Right!...
Here, this is it, "One Summer's Morning", it's not just that
She...' 'Sshh!...Oh! Yes, I see what you mean.' 'It really
Happens, that's just like some of the stuff in the Holbrook
Book I was telling you about, *English for the Rejected*.
The cover's a lovely-looking classic face in profile, with
A pigtail like a child, and a dirty great disfiguring scar
Across her cheek, you're bound to come across it, anyway.' '*I
Looked out of the window / the window that all ways falls*, mmm,
That's chilling, isn't it?' 'Her parents were divorced, but
Her mother's got a new chap. Tracy was caught stealing earlier
This year, it gave me a nasty shock. She's in my form. Look
At this one by the same girl, tell me if, well, just read it,
"The Island".' '...Are you sure she made this up herself?'
'No, she didn't, not all of it...' '*Down to a beach where
The slow waves thunder. / Boom! Boom! Boom!*' 'No, it's here,
I photocopied this from the book she showed me, it's by R.L.
Stevenson, but the changes she made are fascinating, look...'

One Summer's morning

One summer's morning the wind knocked
all the tree's.
The sun shone like a fire the birds
tryed to climb the tree's.
I looked out of the window the
window that all ways falls.
Before a know the sun had rose.
My head had rolled down the road.
the blood dripped down the dran
pipe. the puddle down below the
blood had spread all round the place and
my mother did not know.

The Island

If I have a ship,
I'd sail my ship,
Down to a beach where the slow waves thunder.
Boom! Boom! Boom!
Then I'd leave my ship and Island,
And climb the steeps white with sand,

And climb to the trees,
The coco nut tree on the cliff cliff stand
The birds went fiddle rock slow stop
I they prear down by the side of the road.
The gray blue distant haze
And say myself say Laze Laze pick pick pick,

Tracy

'How did you discover she'd cribbed it?' 'She admitted it,
Well, it wasn't even a confession, she just brought me in
The book to show me. The Director of Education's daughter's
In the same class and she hasn't forgiven me to this day for
Not taking away the "A" I gave her for it... See what I mean?'
'I'm not sure...' 'Well, oh, I forgot to mention that it was
A nonsense poem I'd set them, after reading "Jabberwocky",
But, look, she's turned a loose, repetitive... it's almost
According to Imagist precepts, the way she's dealt with some
Of his lines – *And the grey-blue distant haze! Where the sea
Goes up to the sky* cut to *The gray blue distant haze...*'
'Spare me the prac. crit., please!' 'Well, okay, look at
The last line, *And say myself say Laze Laze pick pick pick*,
Which arose out of *And I'd say to myself as I looked so
Lazily down at the sea*, now, I loved that line before it
Struck me...' 'What struck you?' 'Well, the pastoral Deputy-
Head, Lloyd, he was telling me how he'd caught Tracy red-
Handed nicking from coats during lessons when she'd made
Some excuse to leave the classroom, you know, he'd managed
To work out from a pattern of thefts almost exactly where
And when it was happening, and he actually hid himself
Where he could watch the coat-rack. Imagine, just exactly
As he planned it, Tracy comes out of her lesson – I don't
Know whose, I'm glad it wasn't mine – has a look round her
To make sure the coast's clear, then starts dipping into
People's pockets! Christ, how do you think she felt when
Lloyd appeared?' 'And you think *Laze Laze pick pick pick*
Was inspired by the experience, do you?' 'It's obvious,
Isn't it? Don't you think it's plausible?' 'I'll give you
"Plausible", which may be generous.' 'Well, look at this
One, which...' 'I said *one*, and I've looked at two already!'

After Ten

The light that was failing hours ago
When I went out to bat appears, if anything,
Brighter than it was before the storm.

White Xmas?

They've taken bets on it! But
Who decides? What if drifts
And glassy pavements, thawing,
Blackening, still technically
Christen this Christmas White?

For now we've had every grace
Of snow except a final thaw,
Yet people are saying, 'It's
All right on Christmas cards!'
And stupid things like that –

May their car engines freeze!
(But let it thaw unexpectedly
In St Helens, so that Gill
Can take her driving test,
Then let it freeze up again!)

Father Christmas lost his rag
In Debenhams. He very nearly
Strangled a little boy. Sally
Got hit by a halfbrick of ice:
'It was only a snowball, Miss!'

How Many Streams Can You Rake
With Your Copper Rake?

The nets have come up empty, leaving us free to imagine
What the object was. Who crayoned large, red slogans
On my body as I was sleeping? The dream
Would bleed away if I opened my eyes. This longing
Beyond you is love, and no cause for sadness.

.

Groundless Anxieties

It seems that my decisions have no force;
That nothing is to come of it but this.
The branch crashed into the flooded
Hollows, but no one noticed. The scene
Of the crime, in its beauty, looked
Just as it would in June, as if to attribute
Power or principle to the ghost of a wood.

The Strength of a Rope

Lucidity is good in all things;
In weather, and in the activity
Of an afternoon, harvesting
Irrelevancies. Mum's
Wondering whether a Henry VIII
Stamp won't upset the Catholic
College she's applied to. They
Discriminate against Ulster
Protestants, the priest
At her last interview was
Quite candid about it. Dad
Asked me who said, *Every good
Servant does not all commands*,
He thought it was Talleyrand. I
Was delighted to remember my
Cymbeline, in the end, after
Looking it up in the *Dictionary
Of Quotations*, but in vain.
*The strength of a rope may be
But the strength of its weakest
Part*, but this principle
Does not apply to poetry, as
Augustine Birrell says. I like
His criterion, too: *Do we
Whisper him in our lady's ear?*

The Hedgehog

I've seen so many hedgehogs on evening walks
That tonight I set out looking for one,
Half-humorously putting to the test
The natural thought, that what you look for
You don't find. There were magpies
In the field behind the farm,
And blackbirds looking larger than life –
But by the time I got down to Carr Bridge
I'd almost forgotten about hedgehogs,
For the fields on either side of the track
Were weeks away from harvest. Then,
Coming under the bridge into the first flares
Of a kindling sunset, I saw the field
Was lighter like the grass beneath a tent.
The hay was heaped in a rough diagram
In the middle, and the fear that isn't fear,
But a delicious instinct, alerted me
To the seriousness of the hunt –
But before I had a split-second to investigate
The rounded dark lumps that were probably soil
I had sight of a lump
That was definitely a hedgehog! I hastened
Across the field, but instead of heightening
The tension diminished, for the creature's
Amazing vulnerability amused me, as much
As its innocence in going about its business.
It made more noise in crossing the stubble
Than I did, and I was within
A couple of yards
When it finally stopped sniffling, only
To carry on regardless as soon as I froze.
It was in backing away that I disturbed it.

Torches

'You need a red filter,' Brian said.
'Owls can't see red.'
'I've got a red filter, wait there –
Look at that!'
                     'It's not very bright.'
In fact it was absurdly dim,
And couldn't penetrate the leaves at all,
So Brian got his ordinary torch
And the contrast was ridiculous.
'I paid eight quid for this!'
                           'Well,
At least you've got the filters
And the flash.'
                  'Oh, yeah,
It can do all sorts of tricks
With what little light it produces!'

Long May You Run

'Has Melinda been here?' 'She was here a few days ago.
We drove over from Culcheth. I showed her the house,
But I hadn't moved in at that time, so she hasn't been inside.
Oh, it was funny when I spoke to her on the phone – for a start,
I never expected to get hold of her in the first place,
But before I could gather my thoughts I was talking to her.
She was very casual, you know, she just said, "Oh,
Are you doing anything this week?" and I said, "No,"
So, it was her idea, she suggested coming up for the day
In the little car she's got. It's a Fiat 126.
Gill's got a Fiat 126, incidentally.
I said, "This is too easy, Melinda," and she laughed, you know,
I was amazed, I wasn't thinking, "Where's the catch?" or anything,
I just couldn't believe things could be going so smoothly.
Anyway, she was as good as her word. When she was leaving,
  though –
She could only come up for the day, because she was going down to
  Norfolk
For the weekend, but she promised to come back up
As soon as she got home, and stay for longer. I said, you know,
I couldn't really see it, can you blame me?'
'Is it back on with the minister-to-be?'
'No, she's got another bloke now, he's a teacher too,
At the same place. He's in his thirties. You can't compete
With mature, sexy disciplinarians in their middle-thirties,
Can you? It's not fair, it's cradle-snatching.
What about your romance, the one you mentioned...' 'Uuuh,
I told you about her, didn't I?' 'No. Well, she was at your party,
Wasn't she? But you never introduced her, you just said,
"That was Sal, by the way," the next morning,
When I couldn't even remember what she looked like.' 'Well,
She only called into the party for a few minutes. I thought
You realised who she was.' 'How should I have done?...
What's the situation now, then?' 'Uuh,
Have I bored you with the details?' 'Well...
You said something about her having to have a child
In the next year or two...' 'She's gone back to the bloke
She was living with before.' 'Oh, I suppose it's over, then?'
'A relationship is never finished, only abandoned.' 'Ay,

That reminds me of something in my teaching-practice, at Durham,
This fifth-year girl was insisting that she'd finished her poem
And couldn't do any more with it, so I said, "*A work
Of art*, etc." and she said, quick as you like,
"I've abandoned it, then." I couldn't help laughing,
I mean, it's a pretty good answer, really, don't you think?'

Grebe Lodge

There were fishermen on my stretch of the canal,
So I headed up towards Bickershaw, crossed
Over to the other side of the footbridge,
And found myself among fenced-off stock ponds
With paths leading in every direction,
Fussily sign-posted like a nature reserve.
There was a young couple with a child
In front of me, so I selected
A pathway that led to Grebe Lodge, according
To a very convincing hand. There was a mist
On the channels, and dank, sudden cold. The lodge
Was there all right – it stood out against the dusk,
A log cabin whose entrance smelled strongly
Of turf, and it was empty. What I could see
From the viewpoint, as I knelt
On the wooden seat that skirted the wall
Was, to begin with, half a dozen grebes;
Then I looked over the water
At a slag heap shaped exactly like Ben Bulben
With dense grey clouds above, and below
A perilous shadow on the water, a blank abyss.
I was almost alarmed to see a pair of moorhens
Paddling into it, but instead
They bobbed about like plastic ducks
And thought better. I looked to my left
And there, to my delight, there was a heron,
Hunched a little, looking into the pool.
It straightened with an awkward twist
And leaned forward, then flapped out of sight,
Though probably only a yard or two, behind
The bank that divides the pool from open water.

Extra English

It was a relief to have an amicable lesson
With Jolley and his crowd, if only because
Dot was skiving off again – it just shows
What Tony did to me when he booted her out
Of French! Even Mike has to watch his step
With her when she's in one of her tizzies,
He doesn't raise his voice, he just goes,
'Dot... Dot... Dot'! They love Mike, though.
Even Pilch has a good word for him. No one
Seems to mind the 'playful check' that he
Certainly doesn't hesitate to administer –
Christ only knows how he gets away with it!

Pennington Flash

The sky was overcast, but there were blue spaces
In the cloud, and in the distance was a dull red
Stripe, that included Golborne Colliery, which
Looked like a spinning jenny against the looming,
Life-size workings of Bickershaw.
The estate on this side of the canal
Was in broad daylight, as was the golf course,
And an orange bus, on its way to Warrington.
A sprint carried me almost up to the footbridge
Above Plank Lane, and on the far side I took
The short cut down to the lodge, where I watched
The moorhens. There was no sign of a heron.
I was passing the inlet, listening to the ducks,
When the sun became visible, a shining point,
At first, and then a tiny arc,
Subtended by a yacht, and the next I noticed
It was full to overflowing, while the clouds,
In grey confusion, drifted over the rim.
The golfers were still playing when the crimson
Circle slipped into the poplars, sinking its own
Diameter in sixty seconds flat. I made my way
Across the golf links, finding
The perfect surface easily destroyed,
And when I climbed the footbridge behind
The Sportsman, lights had come on, the Flash
Was dull and misty, distant from the colliery
And the canal, which was level, glazed and turbid
As far as the bend, where it met the glowing
Picture-postcard sky, that seemed to depend on
Every footstep of the mile-long catchment area.

The Bittern

Motionlessness can be a give-away:
Should the reeds be shaken by a breeze
The bittern, which knows better than to freeze,
Adopts instead a calculated sway.

The Rope Works

I put the Brahms on
as soon as I got in.
I'd forgotten how well I knew it,
the first side, anyway,
which I like best.

I told you the situation,
'probably next year',
and I suppose I was more or less
resigned to suspense over the summer.
Dad reckons I should make it clear,
to Woodward,
that I'm unhappy on a 1.
Which, all things considered,
I suppose I am –
at least I'd be a bit demoralised
if he did pass me over in September.
Then again
I'd so much rather
it just happened.

Self-doubt has closed in on me
tonight,
andante moderato.
Not just because of that.
I need you more than you realise, Melinda.
For me
there's no such thing as an old flame!
You love me, in a way, I know you do.
You see right through me, somehow,
always have –
my 'presiding deity',
according to Steve;
my muse,
in fact.

You came, anyway,
if only for a day.
I looked into your room
at eight o'clock –
I hadn't heard you stir,
but was still surprised.
Thanks for the note –
I'll definitely come down
before very long.
I hadn't walked so far along the canal,
at least not in that direction,
under the mills
and as far as Bedford High School,
past Butts Bridge.
The rope works
that burnt down in the winter
fascinated you,
but I was trying to imagine Julian,
and Stantonbury, Diss, and Thelveton Hall,
mythological names from another life,
'a full and satisfying one'.
It sounds it, too.

You put me in mind of a thousand things,
then leave!
You double or halve
my pleasure in all I show you,
intensify or wither
even memories.
Melinda,
blue-stocking, scorpion, femme-fatale!
don't desert me – in memory,
or in the next few weeks, whatever you do.

The Water Station

I watched them gracefully go their separate ways.
The moon had risen, like a map,
Its quiet seas the colour of the sky,
And straggles of red campion
Decreed, whatever happened in the south,
The hawthorn should protect its awkwardness
With emerald.
A wood pigeon deserted, terrified.
It ought to have kept its nerve, nevertheless.

Pied Wagtails
From the Classroom Window

I used to imagine they were rare,
Even though I watched them every day.
So did you, as I was delighted to discover,

Though you knew how common they were,
No more a marvel than a magpie or a plover.
No need to impress yourself led you astray.

Waking Dream

A little light from the landing
Reaches the bedroom, through the glass
Above the door. Dim warmth
Surrounds us, and the wind drops

Below the noise of the fan heater.
You talk to me,
And listen to the night: a car
Approaches, slushes faintly

As it turns, and revs its engine;
A container brakes on Wigan Road;
You slip to the window,
Part the curtains –

As you guessed: the pit
Sombre in the frivolous snow . . .
The canal frozen, the Flash
Doubtless a wilderness already.

The Heron

The sun was white, and set among the snowclouds like a bruise.
A twilight settled over the red mills that I confuse.
It almost frightened me, although I took it in my stride:
A sense of winged depression, like the heron's final glide.

Westleigh Brook

It was clear dusk to one who had been outside,
Doubtless dark already to those who were
About to draw the curtains in brilliant rooms.

Leigh RLFC

It must have led somewhere
all summer.
Autumn sunsets
and hurried winter walks
had drawn me every evening
to the Flash,
but on this first warm afternoon
I felt like going farther afield,
so I took the disused railway
out of town,
past the colliery
towards Hilton Park.
It was fenced with front doors,
which had taken a few knocks.
An old man greeted me
in a Polish accent –
'Nossink to do?'
I smiled and replied
and thought, 'You cheeky sod!'
Easter Monday
finds me lazy and bored
and why shouldn't it?

The First Teal

It was a September
Saturday night,

Dull and cold
And a bit misty.

There were coots
Out on the water,

But I was hoping
To spot an owl

Or something,
After the whinchat

I saw in August,
That I thought

At first was a
Pink sedge warbler.

I got my wish
At the last minute,

As the snipe
Took to the air –

In the pool
Below the hide,

Near a mallard
Twice its size:

A teal,
In eclipse,

At dusk,
Half-asleep.

November Floods

i.m. H.M.S. Sheffield

From where I stood at the rim of the canal
The extent of the flooding was difficult to take in
Until I had worked out exactly what was what –
Where the ground was low there was five feet of water
And the oval fence around the reedbeds
Looked like a massive net pegged out by floats.
It rained all yesterday, and again this morning,
After weeks with a downpour nearly every day,
So I might have expected the Flash to be waterlogged –
But now it looked as though a dam had burst
And turbid water, surging like a tide,
Had clean submerged the footpath and the heath.
The stock ponds, prone to flood at the best of times,
Were joined to a system of lakes in a vast plain
Which stretched as far as the line of oaks,
And everywhere I looked were spilling reaches
Which the screaming gulls had colonised.
It was heavily overcast, and twilight failing,
But then, when only the white-breasted shovelers
Really stood out as they coasted like battleships
Between the rafts of snipe and the topmost reeds,
About half an hour before dark it got steadily
Lighter, as the dense mass thinned in the distance,
And then reamassed beyond that, above the higher
Buildings on the skyline, which were shining;
A clearness drifted westwards like a cloud
And lit the swift advance of Atlantic rain.

The Warning Signs

It never occurred to me that the warning signs
Were no more than a bluff – the right of way
Was straight along the track – there were even
Stiles, now I noticed them, set into the gates!

I don't know how many times I've cut through fields
Or got as far as the farm, only to turn back –
I'd never have dared, for fear of being savaged,
To take the straight way through to the lagoons.

True, the signs said only, *Beware of the Dogs!*,
Nothing at all about private property –
But how was I to know that their short chains
Pulled them up about two yards from the track?

Winter Visitors

There were goldeneye, a drake with swollen cheeks,
And the trim dark form of a duck, like the one you saw,
Jump-diving, staying under long enough
To hinder relocation. From the hide
I watched the drake being mobbed by herring gulls,
And then take flight across to the long spit
Where the Canada geese had settled. The stock ponds
Were frozen solid, and the brilliant ice-line
Was threatening to foreclose on the last preserve,
Frustrated by the warm bodies of a thousand birds.

St Mary's

I got the specimen oral work sorted out
For Dennis's standardisation meeting
Today week – and gave 4G their talk marks:
17 for Lance, as Dennis recommended.
He brought in a rabbit, a small black one
Which he'd caught the previous night,
And skinned it, giving
A fine account and producing
Each tiny organ. It took us
A while to get used to the stench
And a copy of *Great Expectations*
Got covered in shit, but it was worth it.
He told us about 'lamping', his technique,
Where the trick is to look for the colour
Of the eyes – green eyes means just a cat,
Red eyes a fox, but a rabbit
Has white eyes that shine out brightly,
And then it's up to the dogs.
It all reminded me so much of Hughes –
My sixth-formers had seen him on the news,
And better still on *Spitting Image*!
'Rain-Charm for the Duchy' does seem
A bit long-winded, but I dare say
He'll improve, as some fair-minded
Person said in a letter to the *Express*.

Breathing Underwater

When I was beginning to think the game was up,
So late in the day, to distil from anxieties
Something more accountable than dreams
To allay the rational fear of losing ground.
And courage wasn't called for, after all.
It is the one you dream about that counts.
This morning it was like breathing underwater.

Slag Lane

It was overcast, but still warm, almost close,
The familiar, dull pause in the summer's course.
The ducks are in eclipse, and only the song-thrush
And the sedge warblers seem to be singing much.

Snow-Covered Peaks

Mum was fretting all summer for us to have seen
The cottage for ourselves, with our own eyes,
And now we can see why! Those images
Fill the mind after sleep, and a long night's drive –
Of snow-covered peaks from the kitchen window,
Or the wild geese migrating, calling out –
No sign of either, true, but what a prospect –
A huge valley of air, and a clear, cold morning.
The geese are long gone now, the snow only just.

Ben Nevis

The ground rose gently at first, but there the path,
Straight upwards, was its steepest, and the stone steps,
Which I found perfectly placed for a rhythmic march,
Were just too far apart, like paving flags,
For you to take in comfort. 'They never consider
Women when they make these things,' you reasonably
Observed as we stopped to take off yet more clothes.
Like angels' visits, few and far between,
Our rests were certainly not, but I needed them too.

Easter

Easter Monday
never seems
to find me
much at ease.

It has been
a lean time,
for various
reasons.

The weather,
for a start,
high winds
taking all

the pleasure
out of a walk –
and then a
bloody awk-

ward term
ahead – if
it's anything
like the last!

The Willow Tree

*Had I to indicate
Your tact with rooted lives*

I could tell he was more than usually eager
To talk to me on the phone, and I soon realised
That it had nothing to do with my first day,
Although he listened so good-humouredly
That I was rather touched, and taken in –
So when he raised the subject of the willow
In the back garden, all became clear.
Every other year he pollards it,
Always to Mum's dismay, which irritates him,
But this year all he's left is a tarred stump
No higher than a rose bush, and her horror
Has thoroughly alarmed him, strange to say,
Arousing his own doubts. I sympathised.
He must have felt so awful, his green fingers
Stained with the blood of a family favourite,
And inwardly have prayed that the hurt tree
Would cloud the mirror with any sign of life.

Grebe Lodge

I had been there in many moods – the wide water
Had taken as many guises as there are evenings
In as many weeks as all my walks would make,
And that was only the water – what of the skies?

For that was all there was, as often as not:
Skies wide enough to bloom and still be empty,
Whether of birds or clouds, however dense;
Wide water deep enough to reflect the whole sky.

Goosanders

There was a white crowd of gulls,
And the silent widgeon twice

Took to the air with swifter teal
To make higher, wider flights,

But the goosanders are gone
That we saw in the ice.

On Sunday it began to thaw –
Gradually the ice-tide ebbed,

The wind dropped, the sun shone,
But the goosanders are gone.

The Chiffchaff

A single field that I have looked upon

I'd always thought, until that Saturday
When restlessness had turned me out of doors
In the middle of the hottest May for years,
That sunshine was a thing to shelter from,
Like rain – not that I ever minded rain;
Or just to make the best of, like an ache.

Swallows were skimming the green wheat
And woodpigeons were clattering about;
I watched a brilliant yellowhammer sing
And pinpointed a skylark in the blue –
But still I felt the heat as a kind of itch
And would have wished the afternoon away.

A change of heart came like a change of mood.
I'd heard from the tall willows in the corner
Of Crow Wood that's the most awkward to reach
What had to be a chiffchaff in full song –
So after struggling through thorn and wire
I found myself at the edge of a white field

Of cuckoo-flowers – not a buttercup in sight!
Among a thousand butterflies, there were
At least a couple of dozen orange-tips;
Bright grass, and myriads of cuckoo-flowers –
Something about the way they were ankle-deep,
All over the one field, made a different world.

Modified Bliss

i

I'm not sure about our new librarians.
I overheard a couple of them, this morning,
Disputing the title of 'cock o'the lib'ry'! Now,
I wasn't having that, so I put them straight.

ii

Not least of the small, incidental pleasures
Of having the school library to look after
Has been to learn that there is in existence
A library classification system called Bliss,

And a variation of it called Modified Bliss.
I have found teaching English, on the whole,
Despite all its frustrations, to be bliss –
And even at its worst, well – modified bliss!

iii

This is the term
When the best of
A year's work's
Done – a long one,
Beginning in early
August, but split
Up into three by
Holidays, which
Takes the
Necessity for
Sheer endurance
Out of it, leaving
September a blur
As weeks spin by,
October a couple
Of views from
Football fields.

Ante Omnia Musae

Of all the Muses (for they tell of nine),
Melpomene, sweet flowing *Mel.*, be mine!

'You've become very boring, did you know?'
'Alison always used to say I was boring.'
'It's funny how nice people often are.'

'I can hardly believe it about Penny.
Is this her first abortion?' 'Now, Melinda,
There's no point in retrospective malice!' 'Well,
There's no point in malice that just stops, is there?'

'Is Melinda there, please?' 'Oh, Jim, you're never going to
Believe this! What I told you was quite true, but I'm afraid
Lindy telephoned this morning to say that her car is still
Quite unfit to drive all this way, and that she won't be home...'

Late October

The mists have cleared, leaving a sense of height
Among the trees that are still shapely with leaves.

Sunset Breeze

It's nearly eight o'clock, the daffodils
And recently-mown lawns no longer bright,
But the blackbirds are in no hurry to sing
And darkness seems as far away as dawn.

Aspull Common

i

I noticed yesterday on Aspull Common
That it appeared to rise a bit more steeply
And take in more around than I recalled,
But it's astonishing to see how much.

I haven't taken this path very often,
And only a few yards command the view,
But what a lovely one, when I'd have said
I'd no more such discoveries to make.

ii

The alder trees have grown a yard – one summer
Has taken their slight tops above the shoreline
And half-eclipsed the view that I first noticed

Only in time to miss; but then again the same trees,
Rising to define it, half-explain why. It was
Only after five years that I had happened to look.

iii
You can't see water
For birch and alder.
A year ago,
On a May night,

The young saplings
Infringed the view
No more than
Eyelashes the sight.

Carr Bridge

Mists were rising, out of the long grass,
And I could smell wet wheat and hawthorn-blossom.
The moon was a bright bulge in a dim sky.

Nightfall

I'd meant to be home for a quarter to five
To see the soccer results on the teleprinter,
But I stayed out too late, till dusk came on,

Or rather a sense of dusk, for I'd have thought
The sky too light for stars, had it been fine.
As it was, the muddy clouds were closing in.

So when one star appeared in a grey rift
That didn't look like open sky at all
It was just bright enough to bring on night.

Greenisland

Green, clear water at the shore, fog just out to sea.
Two redshanks, a turnstone, and a goldeneye,
White even against the fog, which dulls the gulls.
Oystercatchers in flight toward Carrickfergus.
Darkness and fog, planes late and airports closed,
Street lights from the air and brake lights on the road,
And all I've focused on since I left home
Are these shore birds through Tempie's binoculars.

Death-Suited Visitant

Tempie drove us over from Greenisland. Dad, Uncle Sam, John and I
Had to bear the coffin on our shoulders out of the church,
To the sound of the bell, the rooks in the huge-boled beeches, and
Fog-muffled traffic at the bottom of the hill. I couldn't help
Liking the rector, a fundamentalist, but 'a heck of a nice fella',
According to Dad – I found his ecclesiastical Northern Irish tones,
His High-Church sanctimony, rather fitting. She was, after all,
Devout, to put it mildly. It all went so smoothly, and Betty
Was marvellous. There was the grave, and the coffin was lowered in,
And there was my name on the headstone, my great-grandfather's,
And there was a perfunctoriness about it that was felt by everyone,
A sad occasion but not a painful one. She had outlived her own life,
And no-one could still have been 'close' to an old lady so far away
In gentle senility. Dad's cousins and aunts were out in force,
And it was nice to see people I hadn't seen for anything between
Six and twenty-six years. Such as Una, whom I recall a very pretty
Woman of maybe thirty, with two young daughters. She's still pretty,
But fifty-odd. And Henry Semple, whom I'd never met, only heard
     of,
But I recognised him from a photo, with Dad, in Indian feathers,
Aged maybe eight or nine. Here he was, small and dapper, still fairly
Dark-haired, looking younger than his sixty-odd years, a whole
Lifetime later. And John and I were alike, but for John's hairstyle,
Which Julie liked a lot – and Melinda actually fell in love with him
The day we went to the Oxide, the four of us! Or so she says.
But I wouldn't put it past her – she did say he was 'amazingly
     handsome',
'Much better looking than you are'! We shared the floor in Auntie
Eileen's spare room – both of us slept very uncomfortably, but
It was only for one night. Eileen reminded Mum how there had been
Keerys everywhere when they were kids, before she ever knew Dad.
A very Lisburn name. But for me Northern Ireland is memories of
Walking between Warren Park Gardens and Long Stone Street, of the
Football results in the *Belfast Telegraph*, and the Falls Road Baths.

East Bay

The calls and flight sounds of the water birds,
And their swift silhouettes, lulled me awake.
The evening star was crescent, like a new moon.

Dream-Children

Light by five already, no, more like by six –
The clock's ten minutes fast, it's still pitch dark –
But listen to those dratted blackbirds' shrieks!

A bright March evening, after heavy showers,
Brings out a crowd of midnight daffodils –
Daffodils and children, friends' and ours.

Your Sister's Good Hair

1	Edward Byrom to John Byrom	September 16th, 1709
2	Edward Byrom to John Byrom	November 7th, 1709
3	John Byrom to John Stansfield	December 17th, 1709
4	John Byrom to John Stansfield	December 21st, 1711
5	John Byrom to Edward Byrom	July 28th, 1712
6	Sarah Brearcliffe to John Stansfield	October 4th, 1712
7	John Byrom to his Family	April 27th, 1713
8	John Byrom to John Stansfield	March 7th, 1714
9	John Byrom to John Stansfield	September 26th, 1714
10	John Byrom to John Stansfield	May 3rd, 1715
11	William Shrigley to Edward Byrom	August 9th, 1715
12	Edward Byrom to John Byrom	August 17th, 1717
13	John Byrom to Edward Byrom	January 3rd, 1718
14	John Byrom to John Stansfield	January 21st, 1718
15	John Byrom to Edward Byrom	May 3rd? 1718
16	John Byrom to John Stansfield	June 12th, 1718
17	John Byrom to Edward Byrom	July 17th, 1718
18	John Byrom to John Stansfield	April 17th, 1721
19	John Byrom to Elizabeth Byrom	July 18th, 1723
20	John Byrom to Elizabeth Byrom	July 25th, 1723
21	John Byrom to Phebe Byrom	August 27th, 1723
22	John Byrom to Elizabeth Byrom	November 10th, 1723
23	John Byrom to Elizabeth Byrom	December 14th, 1723
24	John Byrom to Elizabeth Byrom	February 20th, 1724
25	Advertisement in the *Post Boy*	February 29th, 1724
26	John Byrom to Elizabeth Byrom	March 4th, 1724

Edward Byrom to John Byrom
September 16th, 1709

I wrote to you by Mr Brookes, and sent you a piece of gold.
Yesterday I received yours of 27th of last month; it hath not come
Directly, and this is, I suppose, the letter I blamed you for promising
And not sending, in mine by Mr Brookes. As for your wig,
Let us know whether you will have it a natural one,
Or wherein you would have it differ from such as Mr Banks wears,
Or Mr Edmonds, Mr Worsley's tutor. I took it as a piece of
    extravagancy
The giving a guinea for altering the last in London, and no doubt
But you were cheated, and worse hair for your own put in. So I say
Write to us when you have noted those gentlemen's wigs
Wherein you would have yours differ, and we will venture it,
So you may be sure of your sister's good hair, and no cheat.

Edward Byrom to John Byrom
November 7th, 1709

Dear son John: It is a long time since I wrote to you, nor have you
Often to me since your last going. I lately brought home Mr Melling
And Mr Worsley from evening prayers, to drink a dish of tea
In your remembrance; they both gave their service to you.
Mr Melling intends to go into orders next ordination at Chester,
And Mr Worsley I believe will get a good curacy. Good son, look now
Before you to consider how precious your time is, and how
To improve yourself; to consider the end proposed in your education,
To fit you for sacred orders. I am satisfied from Cousin Harper and
Merchant Taylors, and now your tutor, that God hath given you parts,
And I have no reason to suspect your conversation. I do but write
By way of admonition, because fine parts, if set upon good subjects
And proper means to good ends, will grow and be admired,
But set upon unprofitable notions, will be very impertinent. Whence
Have come all the heresy and heretics in the church but from men
Of parts? And the most ingenuous have need of the word and grace
Of God to instruct and guide them; whatever books you read, be sure
To read Dr Hammond on the Psalms and Lessons, with Dr Whitby,
Every day; it is not every young scholar hath them, but you have,
And shall want no necessary thing I can buy you. My brother Byrom
Is so lame of the gout, he cannot go to London this year, and only
Cousin Thomas goeth; it is much upon him so young, but he is a good
Lad, and will do his best. Dear John, thou art much in my love
And in my care, and I hope God will give me comfort in thee. I have
Written you here a long letter, to make amends for long silence.

Your very loving father, E.B.

John Byrom to John Stansfield
December 17th, 1709

We had a sermon preached at our St Mary's on the 5th November
By Mr Edwards of St John's, which was refused to be licensed,
But printed by him at London. I never heard of it before
I saw the advertisement last night, but will buy it
To see why our University refused to license it. Do you think
The Church out of danger, or no? Or that people are better or
Worse than in Queen Elizabeth's days? Or what comparison
Is there, between the state of the Church in that reign and this?
Is the *British Apollo* put down? Or do you take in the *Tatlers*,
Which are mightily admired here, or know you the author? Take
Your own time to answer me.

Yours, J.B.

John Byrom to John Stansfield
December 21st, 1711

I would fain have nothing hinder the pleasure I take
In thinking how soon I shall change this tattered blue gown
For a black one and a lambskin, and have the honourable title
Of Bachelor of Arts. BACHELOR OF ARTS! John; how great
It sounds! The Great Mogul is nothing to it. 'Ay, ay, sir,
Don't pride yourself upon your fine titles before you have them.
Are you sure of your degree? Can you stand the test of a strict
Examination in all those arts you are to be Bachelor of?
Has not one of your blue gowns been stopped this week
For insufficiency in that point already, and do you hope
To escape better?' Why sir, you say true, but I will hope on,
Notwithstanding, till I see reason to the contrary.

Yours, J.B.

John Byrom to Edward Byrom
July 28th, 1712

Dear Brother: We all give our dear love and service to you,
And shall be very glad to see you and Cousin Sleigh. My
Mother is sometimes better and sometimes worse; she often
Enquires if there be any letter from Neddy, and when he is
Coming down; everybody that knows you is asking me that
Question too, and you will save me a deal of impertinence
If you come soon. If you have not parted with your hautboy
What if you bring it down? It is a brave instrument for
The lungs, and one might attempt it in the country without
Disturbing street or college. Do you know that the new church
Is to be consecrated the 17th instant?
                                Dear brother, farewell. – J.B.

Sarah Brearcliffe to John Stansfield
October 4th, 1712

Brother John is at Kersall; he goes out every night and morning
Down to the water side, and bawls out one of Tully's orations,
So loud they can hear him a mile off; so that all the neighbourhood
Think he is mad, and you would think so too if you saw him.
Sometimes he thrashes corn with John Rigby's men, or helps them
To bring potatoes in, and works as hard as any of them. He is
Very good company, and we shall miss him when he is gone, which
Will not be long to now; Michaelmas term is very near beginning.

John Byrom to his Family
April 27th, 1713

Honoured mother, dear brother and sisters: How do you all do?
I write by Mr Wilcoxson's man, who brought Mr Hooper's books
And clothes, but nothing for me; you having, I suppose,
Deferred sending my cargo till his next journey. Dr Clark's
Book, which you so deservedly admired, – it is my fortune that
I must dispute against it next month in the Bachelors' Schools,
I being in the combination for an opponency to one of our year,
A Fellow of Caius College, who has chosen to defend Dr Clark,
And one Eugenius, who asserts the planets to be inhabited;
Therefore if sister Dorothy or any of you can lend me
An argument or two to prove either of these philosophers
Deficient in his hypotheses, I shall be obliged to you. My
Antagonist is in orders. There is one Law, a M.A. and Fellow
Of Emmanuel, has this last week been degraded to a Soph.,
That is, the year below a Bachelor, for a speech on a public
Occasion reflecting, as is reported, on the government, &c.
He is much blamed by some, and defended by others; but he is
Said to be a vain, conceited fellow.

Your dutiful son, loving brother and humble servant, J.B.

John Byrom to John Stansfield
March 7th, 1714

Thursday we buried Dr Smith, one of our Seniors and Vice-Master,
So now we have three Fellowships, and one of my Seniors
Is going to be made Fellow of another college. But this oath –
I am not satisfied so well as to take it, nor am I persuaded
Of its being unlawful. May I not rely on the judgment
Of thousands, thousands good, pious, learned men,
For its being a lawful oath? It is very hard –
Everything so orderly settled in regard to posterity,
And must all be undone for the sake of a man who has a disputed
Title to his birth and right too. I saw a book in our library
The other day, where the Pretender's birth is made very suspicious,
And all your affidavits, allegations, &c., made nothing of.
I suppose you have seen the book, what say you to it?
How is it likely this young fellow should ever come amongst us?
The Queen and Parliament have settled the succession in a Protestant
Family, and made what provision they can for our religion and
    liberties,
And why must we not be content? Though, for what I hear, few are
    otherwise.

Yours, J.B.

John Byrom to John Stansfield
September 26th, 1714

Dear John: How do you do? 'Nay, how do you do?' you'll say. Nay,
I'm in a poor condition as to a Fellowship. All our competitors
Are come, so we are really eleven. My Lord Halifax's favourite
Rid post to take a Fellowship among us yesterday, and that Lord
Will be declared Lord High Treasurer tonight; and who dares
Disoblige him? His coming has spoiled the little hopes
We unsure men had. I am writing my epistles over to present
To the Master and Seniors tomorrow; then Tuesday and Wednesday
And Thursday, we are examined; Friday thrown out – alas, poor us!

Yours, J.B.

John Byrom to John Stansfield
May 3rd, 1715

Dear John: I received yours, indeed I wanted to hear from you.
Our Vice-Chancellor has forbid the coffee-houses taking in
Any other papers but the *Daily Courant, Evening Post, Gazette,*
&c., so that our written letters, *Post Boy, Flying Post,*
Examiner, Spectator, &c. are all banished, and we must have
News without politics. The abjuration oath hath not been
Put to us yet, nor do I know when it will be; nobody
Of our year scruples it, and indeed in the sense
They say they shall take it, I could; one says he can do it
And like the Pretender never the worse; another that it means
Only that he won't plot to bring him in, he doesn't trouble
His head about him, &c. Do not all your lawyers, divines here,
Doesn't the Church of which we are members, in her prayers
And practice, in effect declare it lawful? Did we not swear
To the Thirty-Nine Articles, Doctrine of the Homilies, &c.,
And have you read all the Homilies? You know my opinion:
I am not clearly convinced that it is lawful, nor that it is
Unlawful – sometimes I think one thing, and sometimes another.
This same Cambridge is a sad Whiggish place.

Farewell. – J. Byrom

William Shrigley to Edward Byrom
August 9th, 1715

Dear Sir: I received your last, and thank you for your trouble,
But especially for the news part, which at this time is very
Obliging. As to Manchester, matters stand thus. Major Wyville
Went the 8th for Halifax, and took along three of the six
Troops of dragoons. The commandant at present is Col Foley,
Who seems a very modest gentleman. We whigs intend
To dinner him and supper him round, and thus by degrees to
Make him our own – though Major Wyville cost us damnable dear!
On Monday, when the Major went, some Millgateers were so rude
As to shout 'Down with the Rump!'; the colonel has got a man
Who was seen amongst 'em; he lives at the Duck in Deansgate.
There's talk he was offered the fiery trial to make him
Confess who had set him on; they named him Trafford, Pigot,
Shrigley, and more besides, but the rascal was hard. We whigs
Are in great fear of the Pretender, for really, to say true,
We have carried things to that height since King G. came over
That the tories will be apt to remember us, and God knows
They are twenty to one here. 'Tis whispered that several more
Great ones are for going after Ormond; have you heard? The
Tories are hearty, don't run away, and seem no ways dejected,
Which occasions various speculations. Perhaps, ere this reach
You, some great news may be stirring; let's hear it.

Yours, NNNN

Edward Byrom to John Byrom
August 17th, 1717

Dear Brother: Yours of the 8th and 13th, inst. are come safe to hand,
And have much rejoiced us all, for some of my sisters had almost
Given you up. That you are well is all we wanted to know,
And now you are fixed, let us hear often from you,
As you shall from us, and be not in too much haste to come home.
I hope you have improved yourself in physic; I would gladly have you
Employ yourself that way; and you need not doubt of our
    encouragement.
Not one person but ourselves knows where you are, but we think
    now to
Let our friends know that you are studying physic at Montpelier.
You may save yourself any trouble of enquiring after Mr Roberts;
He is hereabouts, but thinks himself excepted from the Act of Grace,
As are all persons who have gone beyond seas, or all who have been
With the Pretender. There is no providing any passage for you
At this distance; you may take your chance when you come to
    Bordeaux,
If you come that way. Mother sends her blessing, and we all our love
And services. Fail not to write often, and you shall hear again from

Your loving brother, Edward Byrom

John Byrom to Edward Byrom
January 3rd, 1718

Sister Phebe writes me word that Mr Lesley, your library keeper,
Is going to die; that the feoffees ask if I will have the place.
I could like it very well, but I suppose it tied to certain
Engagements which I do not like so well; I suppose the feoffees
At liberty to give it to one in or out of orders,
But whether he must take the oaths or no perhaps
Depends not upon them. You all invite me home very kindly,
And in spring I think to come to you by way of Paris.
I have nothing should tempt me from your company at present
But the occasion of a little insight into physic in this place.
Pray duty to my mother. I often wish myself walking with her
Here, this fine winter. I have been too long without writing,
But I hope you will not revenge yourself that way, but write to
Your ever loving brother and servant,

J.B., Dr of Physic

John Byrom to John Stansfield
January 21st, 1718

Dear Landlord: How do you do? I hope to have the satisfaction
Of seeing you all in the spring, which I now begin to long for.
There was here a while ago a thesis defended upon the question
That voyaging was good against melancholy; seeing the physical
Doings here has invited me to turn my thoughts that way during
My stay here, and I am come to wish I had always thought of it.
If when I come amongst you I meet with opportunities
Of improving myself therein, I should be glad to go on in that
Road. Why won't you let's have your advice thereon? 'Tis an
Odd sort of winter we have here with us; in England one should
Call a fine spring; but indeed this Montpelier is a very happy
Climate. I intend to send some of my future patients over here
For a change of air; and I wish I could blow you over a cellar
Full of our wine that we have for threepence a great bottle.
Pray let me know whether you would have me turn doctor. I wait
For the pleasure of hearing from you, and am

Votre très humble serviteur, J.B.

John Byrom to Edward Byrom
May 3rd? 1718

Dear Brother: The post is this minute a going out,
So I run to the coffee-house to return you answer
In haste to yours, and let you know that I should
Be very willing to have the Library, and am very
Much obliged to you for your pains in engaging
The feoffees; if you can be sure of it, let me
Know further; it will be better worth while than
Staying for a doubtful chance of a fellowship,
Whose profit will be slow a coming. Besides, 'tis
In Manchester, which place I love entirely. Clock
Strikes. –
      Yours, J.B.

John Byrom to John Stansfield
June 12th, 1718

Dear John: I was sadly surprised with yours, concerning
The loss of your little son, when I was expecting far
Other news. You will believe me to be very much grieved
Without my telling you so. I should be more concerned
On your account if I was not well persuaded that you
Would reason yourself into as great patience as nature
Might permit. He that gave him to you hath taken him to
Himself, Whose goodness leaves no doubt that it is
Better for you both; and your affliction, though great,
Hath noble alleviation. Perhaps it may still please God
To give you a son to stay with you. I heartily wish it
So, if He think fit, and shall rejoice in doing for him
What his brother is indeed too happy to want.

Your loving friend, J.B.

John Byrom to Edward Byrom
July 17th, 1718

Dear Brother: I ask your pardon for long silence all this while,
But I had nothing new to acquaint you with save what relates to
Mr Stansfield, who I thought had himself told you that his wife
Was brought to bed of a son on Midsummer day, to whom I stood
Godfather and called him John. The poor infant has had the same
Fate with his two brothers of that name, being but eighteen days
Old when he died of a thrush. I have been amusing myself
With the case of this child, (and indeed his two brothers,) how
Being in all appearance born healthful, and thriving for some
Days after its birth, it should be thus carried off; but
Whatever thoughts I have of the matter I may keep 'em to myself,
For how should a young doctor dare to dispute with an old nurse?

Yours, J.B.

John Byrom to John Stansfield
April 17th, 1721

Dear John: I thought to have written a long letter in answer
To your last, but when I had mustered up all the philosophy
I was master of, I thought you would perhaps think it was
Like my praising potatoes over a good rump of beef. What
I should say to you now you would consider the unexperienced
Ramble of a man who, having all the happiness in the world
Fallen into his lap at once, had no notion of the weight
Of misfortunes; and yet, if you persist in your uneasiness,
I will try, though I lose my pains, if I cannot reason you
Out of it; though 'tis very hard to convince a man that does
But barely exist that 'tis possible to be happy! My friend,
I know misfortunes make us dull; but I know too that they
Ought not to do so; that we are obliged to use all efforts
In nature not to frustrate the intention of wiser, kinder
Powers. But I only design now to ask you how you do, not
To talk to you about these things wherein you are fitter to
Be my master. I shall look to hear from you. Don't believe
I shall ever be too busy for your correspondence – I love it
Too well. My wife's and mine to you and yours, –

J.B.

John Byrom to Elizabeth Byrom
July 18th, 1723

My dear love: How dost thou do? I presume our friend Robin
Is arrived on your coasts, if he have not eloped from his
Fellow travellers. I had a deal to do to bring him off,
But, being obliged by my profession to finish an adventure
If I once undertake it, I bounc'd through the difficulties
That stood in my way, and carried my damsel away with me
Safe beyond Highgate. I pity them for the concern
They have been in about him, and wish them more joy from
His future conduct. I have lost a handkerchief, picked out
Of my pocket, a white one; I never saw the like, there's
No tenting them, do what one can; I wish you would send me
A silk one or two. Dear love, dear baby, good night,
Though 'tis hardly night yet. I am going to dress for the
Royal Society. How dost thou like the hedgehog on my seal?
Is it not a stout one? Write again soon to thine and Bet's,

J.B.

John Byrom to Elizabeth Byrom
July 25th, 1723

My dear love: How do you do? Mr Lever and I came hither from
    Windsor
Yesterday evening; Mr Haddon brought us from Oxford as far as that
Same place. The Vice-Chancellor subscribed for two books, and three
More of Brasenose, and three more promised; in other colleges
    nobody,
But after some while I presume I shall have some of 'em; they wisely
Take time to consider of so serious an affair as half a guinea.
The thing is, they don't seem to be over curious at my aunt Oxford's.
I can't say that coming to London ever appeared less agreeable to me
Than it does now; but indeed I never had before those tender
Engagements which you and Miss Betty have brought on me. How
    does my
Little wench do? Be sure, my dear, do not fail to write to me by the
Next post, for though I am as easy as I can while absent from you,
I would have the pleasure of knowing how you do, as often as I could.

Thine, thine, thine, J.B.

John Byrom to Phebe Byrom
August 27th, 1723

Dear Phebe: How do you do? I have not time to answer yours,
Or else I should; will you help me to answer this famous
Challenge? You see, Mr Weston has quite spoiled my project;
I am forced to run away, to come and get some of your help.
You cannot think how glad I am that I shall see you all
Again so soon; it will comfort me so much that I think
I shall not be so afraid of this great giant in shorthand
That threatens such victories over me. Here I am very busy
And yet very idle; but you are not to think it is anything
But a certain sort of necessity that obliges me to be
Absent for so long from my dear wives both.

Yours, J.B.

John Byrom to Elizabeth Byrom
November 10th, 1723

My dear love: Being in Jo. Clowes's chamber all alone this afternoon,
And pretty well tired with my journey, I take his pen and ink
To divert myself with writing to thee. I thought I must have stayed
At Northampton two or three days before I could have got any further,
I was so very much fatigued, and such a pain in my side, not so much
With the length of the way, for we had come but forty-four miles,
But with the awkward little hobbling horses I met with; my right arm
Is sore with whipping them and hagging them along; but the night
Recovered me enough to ride again, and we made two days,
    Northampton
To London, whither we might have got as soon upon our own horses,
And saved much hurry and expense, but thank God we got here
Safe and sound at last. I hope in a little while to send thee word
Of better luck than I enjoy at present. I am aweary with writing all
This nonsense, which be sure burn when thou hast read it. I see I am
Like to have business enough on my hands, and a task hard enough
To carry my point; but I must not be discouraged. Well, farewell, my
Bets both.
      Yours ever, J.B.

John Byrom to Elizabeth Byrom
December 14th, 1723

My dear love: I had thine last post, and am glad all friends are well.
Dr Smith is come to town tonight. Dr Bentley and I went to
     Bishopsgate
To meet him in the coach, but were a few minutes too late. In our way
We got some of Weston's new challenges, which are given away
At his stationer's in Cheapside. I am not yet inclined to take notice
Of this furious antagonist, which, if I do not, he says, I am told,
That he will press me further. I shall be sorry to be forced
To answer him, but if people's not considering the matter justly
Shall oblige me to it, I must submit to that stupidity. This fellow's
Nonsense does harm at present, but I think it will rather be
Serviceable to our design at last. I cannot determine whether to come
Down with your sister or no. How should I? I must not trifle about my
Project; all the burden lies upon my shoulders only, and I must
Bear it. I write in Peter Leycester's chambers, and he has come in,
And bids me give o'er; it is indeed late. Let me hear from thee, love,
As oft as you can spare time.

                                      Your affectionate husband, J.B.

John Byrom to Elizabeth Byrom
February 20th, 1724

My dear love: Yesterday I received thine by Mr Chetham,
Who came here about three; so I am removed to 'Squire
Joseph's till he goes back again to Manchester. Mr
Hooper and Jo. Clowes have been to pay Mr Weston
A visit, and we have had good diversion in the account;
Frank Hooper's grave countenance prevented suspicion.
He describes me seven foot high, tolerably dressed in
A tie wig, spent my fortune, and a little light-headed;
Showed 'em all his challenge, boasted how he had
Frightened me from dispersing my proposals publickly,
But seems at the bottom to be plaguily afraid. He says
I come to Dick's coffee-house almost every night,
Where he intends to challenge me before the company;
Which when he does I shall let you know in what manner
He molishes me. Poor Bet, she continues well, I hope.
Mr Chetham laughs at my married longings as usual. Thy
Dearly loving husband,

              J.B.

Mr WESTON'S Answers to Mr BYROM his proposals
Being writ in too great Haste and Passion, the Reader
Is desired (If there be any of them left) to correct the
Following Errata:

Paragraph 1. 'Whereas Mr BYROM and his friends
Privately give away at the Lobby of the House of Commons
And other Places Proposals,' &c.: for 'privately'
Read *publickly*.

Par. 3. For 'Mr Smith,' r. *Dr Smith*.

Ibid. 'What is Legum Doctor, &c. to Short-Hand?': dele.
This Query. Mr Weston thought that *Legum-Doctor* had been
Doctor of *Legs*, and so had nothing to do with any *Hand*;
But has since been informed that it is Doctor of *Laws*,
And there is no law which forbids a man to understand
Short-Hand who understands anything else.

Par. 5. For 'Mr Weston's new Method,' r. Mr Metcalfe's
Old Method; it being the very same Mr Weston
Has the honour to teach, with some ingenious Arbitrary
Additions of his own.

Par. 6. 'But to bring an end to the Controversy,' dele.
Controversy; Mr Byrom not having yet entered into any;
And for 'Controversy,' r. *Race*; Mr Weston hoping,
That as he runs by himself, he shall certainly win.

Finally, for 'this Short-Hand Bubble,' r. JAMES WESTON.

John Byrom to Elizabeth Byrom
March 4th, 1724

My dear love: How dost thou do? Since I wrote to thee last,
Nothing extraordinary has happened in relation to my plot;
But I write, however, for writing's sake. On Tuesday
I dined at Mr Ferrand's the apothecary, who I think to have
For one of my receivers in the city; that night I saw some
Of the Royal Society men at their club in Paul's church yard,
But Dr Jurin not being there, (he is at Tunbridge,) did not
Mention it to them the first time I came there. Yesterday
I came to Mr Chetham's chamber in Gray's Inn; the day being
Wet, did not stir out much. Today Mr Lever and I dined with
Mr N. Pimlott at a tavern, and tonight I have been with
Mr Kelsall; he may be of great service, being a favourite
Of Walpole, and acquainted much with the great folk. And this,
You see, is how I go on, dull enough for me to be obliged
To such an absence, but so it must be; I am pretty well
Tired with walking up and down these long streets. My dear,
It is now near ten, and I must go get a mouthful of supper,
Would it were with thee. My love, take care of thyself,
And do not forget thine old acquaintance, lord, and master,
And subject,
        J.B.